ILLUSTRATIONS BY

Ashley Bryan

AND

Jan Spivey Gilchrist

POEM BY

Jan Spivey Gilchrist

HarperCollins*Publishers*

MY AMERICA

Have you seen my country?

Seen my
magic skies?

Seen my

mighty waters?

Have you seen

my land?

Have you seen my country?

Seen my

wings abound?

Seen my

water creatures?

Seen my

beasts

and fowl?

Have you seen my people?

We hail from every shore.

Have you seen my homeland?

Have you seen my country?

Have you seen my AMERICA?

MY AMERICA

Have you seen my country?
Seen my magic skies?
Seen my mighty waters?
Have you seen my land?

Have you seen my country?
Seen my wings abound?
Seen my water creatures?
Seen my beasts and fowl?

Have you seen my people?
We hail from every shore.
Have you seen my homeland?
Have you seen my country?
Have you seen my AMERICA?